SIMPLE
aRT
OF
SUCCESS

380 THOUGHTS TO INSPIRE & MOTIVATE

KATHY WAGONER

SOURCEBOOKS, INC.®
NAPERVILLE, ILLINOIS

Published by Sourcebooks, Inc.
P.O. Box 4410, Naperville, Illinois 60563-4410
(630) 961-3900
FAX: (630) 961-2168
www.sourcebooks.com

Library of Congress Cataloging-in-Publication Data

Wagoner, Kathy.
   The simple art of success: 380 thoughts to inspire and motivate /
   by Kathy Wagoner.
     p. cm.
   ISBN 1-57071-707-9 (alk. paper)
   1. Success—Psychological aspects—Quotations, maxims, etc. I. Title.

BF637.S4 W34 2001
158.1—dc21

                                              2001031319

Printed and bound in the United States of America
         UG 10 9 8 7 6 5 4 3 2 1

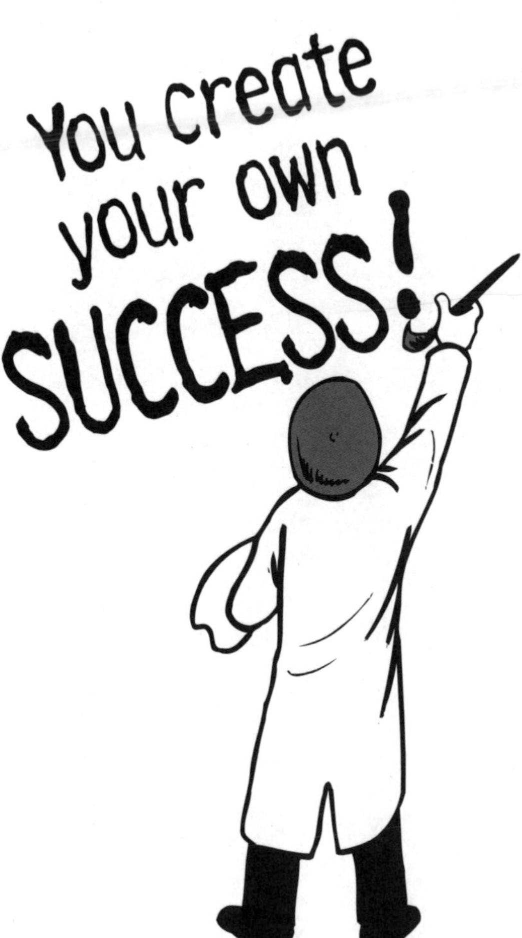
You create
your own
SUCCESS!

Introduction

Believing that you can do what you set out to achieve—garnering resources, taking risks, succeeding— can be an everyday experience. Often, just one bright idea will break up a mental logjam, disrupt emotional trauma, and get you moving in a forward direction again. Here is a collection of quotes and thoughts to keep you moving toward your DREAMS!

Set new goals, start

new projects, and

accept

help from wherever

you can get it.

TAKE THE LEAD—

nobody else can lead for you.

If there is
no wind,
row.

When you get dispirited,
take a deep breath,
give yourself time to recover—
and then—

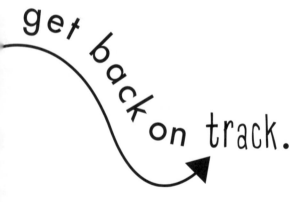

get back on track.

Don't agonize.

Organize

—*Florynce Kennedy*

Just go out there and do what you've got to do.

—Martina Navratilova

Set things up so
that you feel some
sense of achievement
every day.

The secret of getting ahead is getting started.

—Sally Berger

EXERCISE!

Walk to and from appointments.

Take the stairs instead of the elevator.

Go for an evening walk.

Remember,
confidence
comes from practice.

One loses many laughs by not laughing at oneself.

—Sara Jeanette Duncan

ha ha ha ha ha ha ha ha ha ha ha

Think
effectively—
harness
your
mind
to solve
daily
challenges
and

reach your goals.

Be a good, open, honest, driving individual working toward success continually and diligently every day.

I must govern the clock, not be governed by it.

—Golda Meir

Have the courage

to do the

opposite

of what everybody

else is doing

when you think

it's the

right and smart

thing to do.

dreams

Don't be afraid of the space between your dreams and reality. If you can dream it, you can make it so.

—Belva Davis

reality

Be ready for periods of uncertainty and doubt.

Have a general plan for what you'll do to keep your balance.

To attempt to climb—to achieve—
without a firm objective in life
is to attain nothing.

—Mary G. Roebling

Play for the long haul

not for just the
quick payoff.

***Don't
learn
to do,
but
learn
in doing.***

Let your falls not be on
a prepared ground, but
let them be *bona fide*
falls in the rough and
tumble of the world.

—Samuel Butler

Be
"up-spirited"
every day,

playing to adjust,
adapt, and win.

Look squarely at problems, distractions, and obstacles. Come up with **smart solutions methodically** and **rapidly**.

WE KNOW WHAT HAPPENS TO PEOPLE WHO STAY IN THE MIDDLE OF THE ROAD. THEY GET RUN OVER.

—ANEURIN BEVAN

Before a man can manage anything that endures, he must first manage his own mind.

—James Allen

The

Se(ret Of My iNflueN(e

has always been that it remained secret.

—Salvador Dalí

Set goals with a passion and desire to achieve them.

Engage your conscious and subconscious minds.

Logic takes care of itself;

all we have to do is to look and see how it does it.

—Ludwig Wittgenstein

PERSISTENCE,

PERSISTENCE,

PERSISTENCE!

**Bypass
negative people
and negative
influences.**

When you get right down to
the root of the meaning of
the word **"succeed,"** you
find that it simply means
to follow through.

— F. W. NICHOL

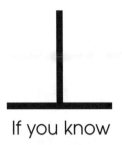

If you know

what you are talking about,

and if you want to convey

that to others,

the words will come.

Even if you're on the right track, you'll get run over if you just sit there.

—Will Rogers

Keep the space around you clean and bright.

Quality is never an accident;

it is always the result of intelligent effort.

—John Ruskin

Accept responsibility for writing your own life's scenario!

Nothing can bring you

peace

but the triumph of principles.

—Ralph Waldo Emerson

Take full **advantage** of the burning genius within you.

Utilize your knowledge and skills.

Learn to reason

forward

and

backward

on both sides of a question.

—Abraham Lincoln

Look into the
eyes of the person
with whom you are speaking.
That says,

*"I really care about what
you are saying."*

Always take a job that is
too big for you.

—Harry Emerson Fosdick

Imagination

is much more important than intelligence.

—*Albert Einstein*

No matter what your job, move toward mastering it. Continually add to your understanding and capability.

All great discoveries are made by men whose feelings *run ahead of their thinking.*

—C. H. Parkhurst

Cultivate mutual respect with the people around you.

There's a mighty
big difference between

good,

sound reasons,

and

reasons that
sound good.

—Burton Hillis

Generate a feeling of

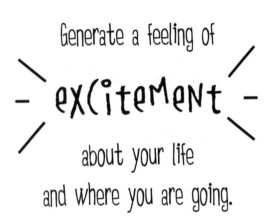

exCiteMeNt

about your life
and where you are going.

is dependent on effort.

—Sophocles

Make it your habit not to be critical about small things.

—Edward Everett Hale

2
3
1

From time to time, reorder your priorities.

The more we **do**,
the more we **can** do.

—William Hazlitt

Let your
hook be
always cast; in
the pool where
you least expect
it, there will
be a fish.

—Ovid

The first step in solving a problem is to admit you have a problem.

Our senses don't deceive us:
our judgment does.

—Johann Wolfgang von Goethe

Got an idea?

Then explain

its benefits

so that

they are

understood

clearly

by others.

Opportunity, sooner or later, comes to all who work and wish.

—Lord Stanley

Daily self-management
is an art.

Only those who have the

patience to do simple things

perfectly will acquire the skill

to do difficult things easily.

—Friedrich Schiller

New approaches

are needed. The problems we

face today are different from

the problems we faced yesterday.

The greater the obstacle, the more glory in overcoming it.

—Molière

You

are the one who must

bring about the results and

outcomes you desire

in life. Nobody else

can do that for you.

YOU MUST HAVE A
clear mental picture
OF THE CORRECT THING
BEFORE YOU CAN
DO IT SUCCESSFULLY.

—Alex Morrison

NOTHING

IS

STRONGER

THAN

HABIT.

—OVID

Persistent
people
begin their
success
where
others end
in failure.

—Edward Eggleston

ENTHUSIASM FINDS THE OPPORTUNITIES AND ENERGY MAKES THE MOST OF THEM.

—HENRY S. HASKINS

Things may
come to those
who wait, but
only the things
left by those
who hustle.

—**Abraham Lincoln**

Clear your mind of can't.

—Samuel Johnson

Learning the art of

talking with others

is only half of the battle.

You need to learn the

art of listening

to them as well.

It is astonishing
what a lot of
odd minutes
one can
catch during
the day, if
one really
sets about it.

—Dinah Maria Mulock

Try

to

be

honest

and

fair

in

everything

that

you

do.

What we earnestly

aspire to be,

that in some sense we are.

—**Anna Jameson**

The difference between

failure and success

is doing a thing nearly right

and doing a thing exactly right.

—Edward Simons

It is

fine

to

if you don't

level them

in the process.

—Walter St. John

Strive for a

creative climate,

one in which you can think, work,

and stretch to be your best.

WISDOM
is knowing what to do next;

SKILL
is knowing how to do it, and

VIRTUE
is doing it.

—David Starr Jordan

All depends on the right use of time. ✓ <u>Prioritize</u> and ✓ <u>organize</u>.

N

E

The great thing
in this world is
not so much where
we stand, **as in
what direction
we are moving.**

—Oliver Wendell Holmes

S

Share your

hopes and dreams.

Others can support you in

making them a reality.

Doing nothing for others

is the undoing of ourselves.

—Horace Mann

When one
door
shuts,
another
opens.

—Spanish proverb

Reason

often makes mistakes,

but

conscience

never does.

—**H.W. Shaw**

How poor they are that
have not patience.

—William Shakespeare

Everything about you—

the way you walk

and talk,

the way you look

and listen—

tells other people what

you think of yourself.

To stumble twice against
the same stone
is a proverbial disgrace.

—Marcus Tullius Cicero

Develop your ability to handle complaints;

it will lead to better relationships.

DISAPPOINTMENT

should always be taken as a

stimulant and never viewed

as a discouragement.

—C. B. Newcomb

HABITS

are at first cobwebs,
then cables.

—Spanish proverb

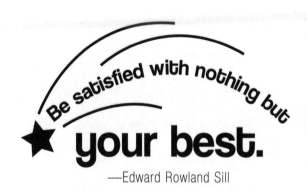

Be satisfied with nothing but **your best.**

—Edward Rowland Sill

Anything one man

can imagine,

other men can

make real.

—Jules Verne

Experience a sense of *excitement* **about yourself and the contribution you are making.**

☑ **Always make sure people are aware of your knowledge and skills, of what you can do specifically for them.**

Much does he gain who learns when he loses.

—Italian proverb

Develop a loyalty

to those you serve.

Be a team player

and everybody benefits.

He who considers too much
will perform little.

—Friedrich Schiller

Truth is the
most valuable thing
we have.
Let us economize it.

—Mark Twain

LUCK

is the chance
meeting of preparation
and opportunity.

From a little *spark* may burst a mighty flame.

—Dante Alighieri

When people inquire
about what you can do
for them, it means
they're **interested** even

before they hear your answer.

You never know

what is enough

until you know

what is

more
than
enough.

—William Blake

Make every contact

a move toward a

good relationship.

is harder than moving.

—Moshe Feldenkrais

Don't let yourself
be diverted from
your duty until you
have finished—
not even if a
cannon goes off
at your elbow.

—Konrad Adenauer

Don't make excuses, make good.

—Elbert Hubbard

Every moment of worry weakens the soul for its DAILY COMBAT.

—Anna Robertson Brown

Here are the criteria for good objectives:

they must be understandable;

they must be challenging;

they must be achievable.

Confidence imparts a wonderful inspiration to its possessor.

—John Milton

Feel the joy of waking up each day. Play your part in life with a sense of fun and confidence.

He who is overcautious will accomplish little.

—Friedrich Schiller

It is impossible
to come to a stop in life.
In every moment, you
are going either
forward or backward.

We lose vigor through thinking continually the same set of thoughts: New thought is new life.

—Prentice Mulford

To expect defeat is
NINE-TENTHS
of defeat itself.

—Francis Marion Crawford

When people pull against one another, the results are harmful for all concerned.

Beware of little expenses; a small leak will sink a great ship.

—Benjamin Franklin

There are imperfections in
every person's life. Do the
best you can with what you
have been given.

Those who trust to chance must abide by the results of chance.

—Calvin Coolidge

There's

no

satisfaction

without a struggle first.

—Marty Liquori

WHEN YOU HEAD OUT

TO SOLVE A CONFLICT, BE

L O O S E—

REALIZE THE SOLUTION

USUALLY WILL BE A COMPROMISE.

Well done
is better than
well said.

—Benjamin Franklin

One of your

purposes in life

should be

to draw out

your own

innate

capabilities

as well as the

capabilities of

those around

you.

SELF-TRUST
is the first secret of success.
—Ralph Waldo Emerson

Be nice to people.

Be courteous.

{ Many times others simply want a sympathetic ear. }

When you have to make a choice
and don't make it,
that is in itself a choice.

—William James

the minute you decide that you want it.

**We may be
personally defeated,
but our principles never.**

—William Lloyd Garrison

**A problem
well stated**

**is a problem
half solved.**

—Charles F. Kettering

To eliminate a problem, you must get to the root of it.

Unless you do that, it will sprout again.

Out of the strain of the doing, into the peace of the done.

—Julia Woodruff

TAKE CARE OF

YOUR BODY

AND YOUR MIND

WILL REAP

THE BENEFITS.

Never give advice unless asked.

—German proverb

THE MORE YOU SAY,

the less people remember.

T H E

F E W E R

T H E

W O R D S,

the greater the profit.

—François de Salignac de la
Mothe-Fénelon

Life's just like advertising:

What you see may
not be what you get.

To carry care to bed
is to sleep with a
pack on your back.

—Thomas Chandler Haliburton

There is always conflict in life.
Learn how to work with it and through it

gracefully.

Be slow of tongue
and quick of eye.

—Miguel de Cervantes

You don't have to live within one model. There is a variety of scenarios, all appropriate for different situations.

Chance

never helps those who
do not help themselves.

—Sophocles

We become what we think about.

—Earl Nightingale

You must look **into** people as well as **at** them.

—Lord Chesterfield

List your advantages on one sheet of paper

and your difficulties on another.

You'll be pleasantly surprised.

Human improvement is from

WITHIN
outward.

—James Anthony Froude

Though brilliant models
of smart behavior can
be found all around us,
we often miss them
—or ignore them.

He who sings frightens away his ills.

—Miguel de Cervantes

The circumstances of others seem
good to us,
while ours seem
good to others.

—Publilius Syrus

Pinpoint your problem.

- Select a course of action.

- Put it into effect.

- Check the results.

Common sense

is instinct, and enough of it is

genius.

—H. W. Shaw

Get on a path of personal growth and continuous study, regardless of your field.

No

necessary

work

can

be

demeaning.

Those who
COMPLAIN
most are most to be complained of.

—Matthew Henry

Love the age you're living in.

**It's the most exciting age of
all recorded history.**

Better bend than break.

—Scottish proverb

You can analyze and reason until you're blue in the face. It's called

"Overthinking."

"Wanting to"
isn't enough. You must

"have to"
if you are going to be a success.

Self-conquest
is the
greatest of
victories.

—Plato

There is a
difference
between
strength
&
power.
You succeed
by developing
the strength
to serve,
not by
cultivating
the power
to dominate.

Conversation enriches the understanding, but solitude is the school of genius.

—Edward Gibbon

Many things
difficult to
design prove
easy to
performance.
—Samuel Johnson

THE WORLD BELONGS TO THE ENTHUSIAST WHO KEEPS COOL.

—William McFee

Habitually

stretch

for the next level—and enjoy the stretching.

An **error** gracefully
acknowledged is a victory won.

—Caroline L. Gascoigne

ADD
A
fresh,
bright polish
TO YOUR
DAILY COMMUNICATIONS.

Is there anyone
so wise as to
learn by the
experience of others?

—François Marie Arouet Voltaire

The

communication

*center is not
in the head;
it is in the gut.*

*It is necessary
to try to surpass
one's self always;
this occupation
ought to last
as long as life.*

—*Queen Christina of Sweden*

Not all tasks are created equal.

Match commitment time **for the task with its** importance.

THE ONLY DIFFERENCE
BETWEEN SUCCESS
AND FAILURE IS
THE ABILITY TO TAKE
ACTION.

—ALEXANDER GRAHAM BELL

**There are very few
things you can't have
if you really want them.**

Consider the

possibilities

**before you
limit your potential.**

Knowledge is of **2** kinds.

We know a subject ourselves,

or we know where we can find information upon it.

—Samuel Johnson

One of your jobs
in life should be
to develop a
feeling of strength
and caring toward
other people.

Politeness

goes far, yet costs nothing.

—Samuel Smiles

**Nothing great was ever
achieved without**

—Ralph Waldo Emerson

An optimist sees an
opportunity in every calamity;

a pessimist sees a
calamity in every opportunity.

—Anonymous

Success is just a matter of **attitude.**

—Darcy E. Gibbons

Peace

rules the day, where
reason rules the mind.

—William Collins

**If
you
go
after
excellence,
you'll
get
it.**

Victory belongs to the most persevering.

—Napoleon Bonaparte

The secret to living, feeling, and acting positively is to

eliminate negative thoughts.

Where there's a will, there's a way.

—English proverb

Take calculated risks.

**That is
quite different
from being rash.**

–General George Smith Patton Jr.

Each morning, set your goals for the day— both **short-term** and **long-term** ones.

CONSCIENCE
is the perfect interpreter of life.

—Karl Barth

The key to

I I

happiness and success in life

**is to find a way to
serve people
well and to uplift one
another constantly.**

A good memory is one trained to forget the trivial.

—Clifton Fadiman

SOLITUDE

is as needful to the imagination as society is wholesome for the character.

—James Russell Lowell

Opinion is ultimately determined by the feelings and not by the intellect.

—Herbert Spencer

Go beyond the normal standards in performance. Dig deeper and put in the extra effort. Work smarter and more *creatively.*

Love
the challenge of
engineering a
task from
beginning
to
end.

Chaos often breeds life when

order breeds habit.

—Henry B. Adams

You are not supposed to

be somebody else.

You are you.

Be authentic; allow yourself to

"become" naturally and gracefully.

Good manners
are made up of petty sacrifices.

—Ralph Waldo Emerson

Add
up
all
of
the
reasons
for
and
against
an
option.

Then, outweigh
the negatives
with solid
benefits before
going ahead.

Vitality

shows in not only

the ability to persist but

the ability to start over.

—F. Scott Fitzgerald

Every day you must

decide what you

could do,

what you

should do,

and what you

must do.

In preparing for battle,
I have always found that
plans are useless, but
planning is indispensable.

—Dwight D. Eisenhower

I am neither an

optimist

nor

pessimist,

but a

possibilist.

—Max Lerner

30 minutes of study a day can make you an expert at something in a surprisingly short time.

First, understand your destructive impulses and weaknesses. Then, get them **under control**.

Patience

and

tenacity of purpose

are worth more than
twice their weight of cleverness.

—Thomas Henry Huxley

Sit down
with a pen
and paper
from time to
time and
playfully
develop your
imagination.

I hope our
wisdom will grow with our power
and teach us that
the less we use our power
the greater it will be.

—Thomas Jefferson

Reluctance or refusal to look at the total situation results in missing an obvious diagnosis.

To instill your ideas in others implies that you know where they should be. Instead, help them see how to get from where they are

to where they want to be.

Character
is much easier kept than recovered.

—Thomas Paine

We are responsible for actions performed in response to circumstances for which we are not responsible.

—*Allan Massie*

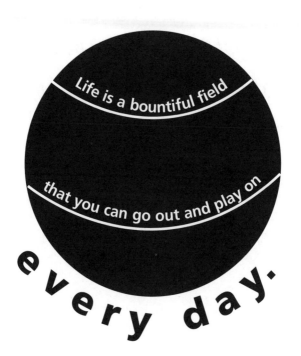

Life is a bountiful field that you can go out and play on every day.

Trust thyself: every heart vibrates to that iron string.

—Ralph Waldo Emerson

If you work at it,
you can swap a
hang-up with a
behavior and way
of thinking that are

OPEN

and

positive.

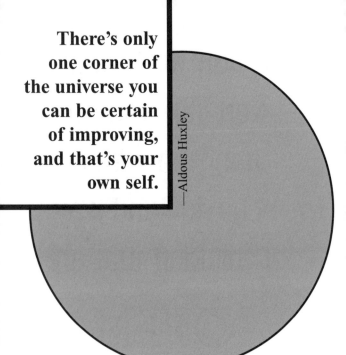

There's only one corner of the universe you can be certain of improving, and that's your own self.

—Aldous Huxley

ALWAYS LOOK FOR THE RIGHT IDEA.

It's there;

YOU JUST HAVE TO FIND IT.

It is characteristic of all deep human problems that they are not to be approached without some

humor

and some

bewilderment.

—Freeman Dyson

Remember,
you are fully human
and you can make mistakes.

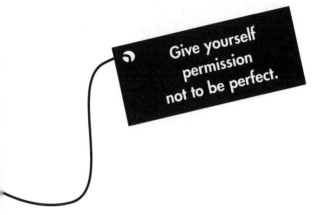

Give yourself
permission
not to be perfect.

PROCRASTINATION
is the thief of time.

—Edward Young

I not only use all the brains I have, but all I can borrow.

—Woodrow Wilson

There are two things to
be considered with
regard to any scheme.

In the first place,
"Is it good in itself?"

In the second,
"Can it be easily put
into practice?"

—Jean-Jacques Rousseau

Apologize
flat
out
when
you
are
wrong
about
something.

The absence of alternatives
demands creativity.

I still need more healthy rest in order to work at my best. My health is the main capital I have and I want to administer it

INTELLIGENTLY.

—Ernest Hemingway

Love yourself.

CHERISH YOUR
DEVELOPING STRENGTHS
AND CAPABILITIES.

The one
self-knowledge
worth having is to
know one's own mind.

—F. H. Bradley

It is easier
to change
a plan than it
is to change a
viewpoint.

To establish oneself

in the world,
one does all one can
to seem established there already.

—François Duc de La Rochefoucauld

Remain **flexible**, **thoughtful**, **receptive**, and ready for every opportunity.

When a thought is too weak to be expressed simply, it should be

rejected.

—Luc de Clapiers Marquis de Vauvenargues

If you are IDLE,
be not **solitary**;
if you are solitary, be not idle.

—Samuel Johnson

The only things you really have CONTROL over are your thoughts.

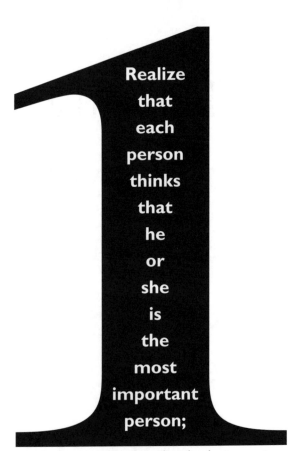

Realize that each person thinks that he or she is the most important person;

respect everyone's individual viewpoint.

No one can build
his security upon
the nobleness of
another person.

—Willa Cather

In this world without **quiet corners,** there can be no easy escapes from history, from hullabaloo, from terrible, unquiet fuss.

—Salman Rushdie

When you get down-spirited from time to time,

take a break *and*
relax.

Keep your eyes on the goal and not on the
stumbling blocks in the way.

start here

If you're getting too many rejections in life, it's time to evaluate your course of action.

A thought which does not result in an action is nothing much, and an action which does not proceed from a thought is nothing at all.

—George Bernanos

Once you have earned a favorable reputation for getting results, you will find people coming back again and again.

Consider new objectives.

Creativity

comes when your mind is

relaxed

and you give it a
chance to probe.

*You must learn to be still in
the midst of activity and to be*

vibrantly

alive in repose.

—Indira Gandhi

It's helpful to work hard—but just as important to work

smart!

It is an
equal failing to
TRUST EVERYBODY and to

TRUST NOBODY.

—English proverb

> **The ablest man I ever met is the man you think you are.**
>
> —Franklin D. Roosevelt

Know how to trap great ideas?

Get them down on paper.

To do what others cannot do is **talent**. To do what talent cannot do is **genius**.

—Will Henry

An idea, to
be suggestive,
must come to
the individual
with the force
of a revelation.

−William James

MANY THINGS CAUSE PAIN

which would cause pleasure if you regarded their advantages.

—BALTASAR GRACIAN

The best preparation for
good work tomorrow is
to do good work

today.

—Elbert Hubbard

Where there is an

OPEN MIND,

there will always be a

new frontier.

—Charles F. Kettering

No matter what
accomplishments you make,

somebody helps you.

—Althea Gibson Darben

Always be on the way to an improved you!

There is nothing
like a dream
to create the future.

—Victor Hugo

HE THAT FEARS NOT
THE FUTURE MAY
ENJOY THE PRESENT.

—THOMAS FULLER

Remember,

there's a time for grinding

out the requirements of the

day-to-day business

and a time for being

imaginative and creative.

The supply of words in the world market is

plentiful

but the demand is falling.

Let deeds follow words now.

—Lech Walesa

Learn your lines
and your
movements and
do them well;
don't lose your
POISE.

The moment of victory is much too short to live for that and nothing else.

–Martina Navratilova

As a man
is,
so he sees.
As the eye is
formed, such powers.

—William Blake

Practice

QUALITY
THINKING

—think through each

step thoroughly

before proceeding.

Resting on your
laurels is as
dangerous as
resting when you
are walking in
the snow. You
doze off and die
in your sleep.

—Ludwig
Wittgenstein

STUDY YOURSELF.

Sometimes you can find ways to eliminate a flaw completely without a total overhaul.

Think big.

At the same time, be able
to be aware of the

smallest details.

It is tact that is golden, not silence.

—Samuel Butler

Aiming for
excellence is
a good idea.
After all, it's
one way to
realize your
own qualities
and how they
can work for
YOU.

To accomplish great things, we must not only act but also dream, not only plan but also

believe.

—Anatole France

Thought

combined with

purpose

becomes

a

creative force.

PROGRAM YOUR SUBCONSCIOUS WITH SHARP, WINNING, AND HELPFUL HABITS.

Trust your gut.

—Barbara Walters

FIND NEW SOURCES OF
INFORMATION.

———

LOOK **high** AND low
in all directions

———

UNTIL YOU GAIN THE
ANSWERS YOU NEED.

What you
persist
in doing
becomes
easier
because
your
power
to do it, and do it
better, increases.

If you have
no confidence in
yourself, you are
twice defeated in the
race of life. With
confidence,
you have
won even
before you
have started.

—Marcus Garvey

Develop good, solid feelings for the

missions in your life.

Become loyal to your goals.

Work first
and then rest.

−John Ruskin

Study the big problems all
the time, but NEVER TO SKIP A SMALL TASK, for one of
the simple duties may hold the
key to the biggest problem.

—John T. Faris

Folks who never do any more
than they get paid for,
**never get paid for any more
than they do.**

—Elbert Hubbard

When good ideas come to you, file them in boxes or folders according to categories.

True contentment

is the power of getting out of any situation all that there is in it.

—Gilbert Keith Chesterton

Get

control

over your emotions—
know when to summon
empathy and how to be
tolerant when you must.

The strongest principle of growth lies in human choice.

—George Eliot

Reach
for
objectives

that will be good for you as well as for those around you.

Nature

does not require that we be perfect;

it requires only that we grow, and we

can do this as well from a mistake

as from a success.

—Rollo May

Take time to understand what is going on in the minds and hearts of those you encounter.

NEVER STOP

searching or researching.

● ● ● ● ● ● ● ● ● ● ● ● ● ● ● ● ● ● ● ●

If you do,

that's when

you also

stop

GROWING.

I know of
no more
encouraging
fact than
the unquestionable
ability of man to
elevate his life by a
conscious endeavor.

—Henry David Thoreau

Character

is

singularly

contagious.

—Samuel A. Eliot

Do the job so well that even your toughest critic—YOU— can take pride in the results.

Let no man
imagine that
he has no
influence.

—Henry George

**Nobody
can
inspire
who
does
not
have
deep
convictions.
They
are
the
results,
but
also
the
feeders,
of
the
spirit.**

—Robert Ulich

Do things in
such a way
that you feel a
sense of
belonging, that
you are a key
player, and
that you are
sincerely
appreciated.

The course of true anything never does run

smooth.

—Samuel Butler

Be sure you are able
to deliver when you
say you will deliver.

That's what education means—
to be able
to do what
you've never done before.

—George Herbert Palmer

No experiment is ever
a complete failure.
It can always
be used as a
BAD EXAMPLE.

—P. Dickson

Life

is occupied
both in
perpetuating
itself and in
surpassing
itself.

—Simone de
Beauvoir

**No matter
what you do,
turn
in an
outstanding
performance.**

There is more
to life than
increasing
its
speed.

—Mahatma Gandhi

Ideas

are a lot like stacks of paper

shuffled around in an office—

some are to be filed for ready

access; some are on the top of

the pile ready for your action.

The man who removes a mountain begins by carrying away small stones.

—Chinese proverb

Think positively.

The
spirit
of man is
stronger than
anything that
can happen
to it.

—Robert Falcon Scott

Don't hurry—

mistakes cause more problems. Instead, proceed methodically, logically, and carefully.

Delegate!

It can save your life—
or, at the very least,
your SANITY.

In making a

living today,

many no

longer leave

any room

for

life.

—Joseph R. Sizoo

The present
is always
determined by
the past, and
always we are
free to
determine
the future.

–H. J. Forman

**Foster a
climate
conducive to
PROBLEM
SOLVING.**

The
future
that we study
and plan for
begins today.

—Chester O. Fischer

PINPOINT

TIME WASTERS.

Determine their methods and
decide how to avoid them.

To fall
into a
habit
is to
begin
to
cease
to be.

—Miguel de Unamuno

300

TO LIVE
HAPPILY
WITH OTHER
PEOPLE, ONE
SHOULD ONLY
ASK OF THEM
WHAT THEY
CAN GIVE.

—TRISTAN BERNARD

An idea

is the most

exciting thing

there is.

–John Russell

It is never too late to
be what you might
have been.

—George Eliot

Always ask questions of yourself:

Where do you want to go?

What is standing in your way?

What do you need to reach your goals?

Be
on
your
toes—
and
work
hard
at
staying
there

every day.

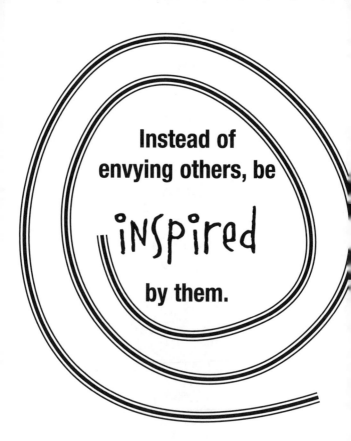

Instead of envying others, be *inspired* by them.

Overcome objections

by first listening to them carefully and sincerely.

Be the change that you want to see in the world.

—Mahatma Gandhi

☑ Don't clutter your desk. Rather, establish a logical flow of items to accomplish in order of priority.

Be your own coach—you know best how to motivate yourself into giving a top-level performance.

Wisdom begins in wonder.

—Socrates

Moderation
in all things is
vitally important.

If you serve others well, you will see a ripple effect: a radiation of good results spreading everywhere, in every direction.

Don't tell your subconscious that you **can't** do something or else it will say,

"Okay."

THE IMPORTANT THING IS TO NOT STOP QUESTIONING.

—ALBERT EINSTEIN

*Everyone
has a fair
turn to be
as great as
he pleases.*

—*Jeremy Collier*

Never deceive yourself or anyone else in any way!

The hardest thing to
learn in life is which
bridge to cross
and which to
BURN.

—David Russell

Make a
COMMITMENT
to be a
professional,
no matter how
big or small the
task may be.

The human being never has the time to be. He only has the time to become.

—Georges Poulet

Dreams

ARE THE
TOUCHSTONES
OF OUR
PERSONALITY.
—HENRY DAVID
THOREAU

YOU ARE THE

outcome of your thoughts.

THE

objectives you desire

WILL ACTIVATE YOUR THINKING

ALONG THAT COURSE.

When you treat others with esteem, their self-esteem grows stronger.

Do what you can
with what you have
where you are.

—Theodore Roosevelt

The
ability
to
beat
the
odds
lies
within
us
all.

Set clear-cut goals;

nurture an active, probing,
open mind;

cultivate deeply felt desires:

you will direct your destiny.

Only those who
risk going

TOO FAR

can possibly find out
how far one can go.

—T. S. Eliot

We often think of compromise as a dirty word,

but actually, compromise can be a fine way to solve problems.

TO SEE
THINGS IN
THE SEED,
THAT IS
GENIUS.

—LAO TZU

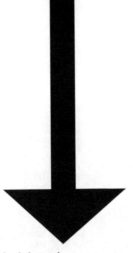

Sketch out every way
imaginable to sell yourself.
**And all the while,
keep searching for even more ways.**

When you
reach the
end of
your rope,
tie a knot
in it and
hang on.

—Thomas Jefferson

We
are
all
lumpy
with
talent.
The
trick
is
to
release it.

—Eric Hoffer

When things
are going well,
don't be afraid to feel
exuberant!

WHAT

WE

SEE

DEPENDS

MAINLY

ON

WHAT

WE

LOOK

FOR.

—John Lubbock

Recognize that defeat is temporary.

Bounce back.

Some
people
are always
grumbling
because roses
have thorns.
I am thankful
that thorns
have roses.

—Alphonse Karr

To turn a good idea into a habit, keep using it until it becomes a **reflex**.

Yesterday is not ours to recover, but tomorrow is ours to win or lose.

—Lyndon B. Johnson

Be innovative.

It's amazing what can happen if you constantly think about how to do things more effectively.

STRETCH YOUR MIND

with exciting new objectives
even though the way to
achieve them may not be
immediately apparent.

EMBRACE THE CHALLENGE OF KEEPING YOUR KNOWLEDGE, SKILLS, AND ABILITIES SHARP AND GROWING.

A place for everything,

everything in its place.

—Benjamin Franklin

Always be flexible,

ready to
take full
advantage
of any
opportunity
that comes
your way.

Act as though it is

impossible

to fail.

I have not failed.

I've just found

10,000

ways that

won't work.

—Thomas Alva Edison

Resist every temptation to sink into a degrading or undermining emotion.

Deliberately
do that
which
is
difficult.

Think sideways.

—Edward de Bono

Confidence comes from competence.

You miss
100%
of the
shots you
never
take.

—Wayne Gretzky

The

secret

to

success

is

directed

effort.

Be innovative,
inventive,
*and never let
an opportunity
slip by.*

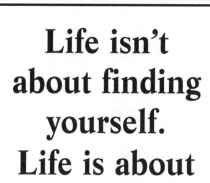

Life isn't about finding yourself. Life is about creating yourself.

—George Bernard Shaw

Be aware that your facial expressions tell others how you feel even when your words do not.

TIME

IS THE
SCARCEST
RESOURCE;
UNLESS IT IS
MANAGED,
NOTHING
ELSE CAN BE
MANAGED.

—PETER DRUCKER

Things should
be made as
simple
as
possible,
but no simpler.

—Albert Einstein

Always work

(reatively

**to build up
and not**

COMPETITIVELY

**to break
down.**

ALWAYS BEAR IN MIND

that your own resolution to succeed is more important than any other.

—Abraham Lincoln

The difference
between

success

and

failure

is the energy and
talent that you give
to a task.

A mind that is
stretched
by a new experience
can never go back
to its old dimensions.

—Oliver Wendell Holmes

the
key
skill
in
approaching
any
situation
is
the
ability
to
ask
the
right
questions.

AN OBSTACLE IS

SOMETHING YOU SEE

WHEN YOU TAKE YOUR

EYES OFF THE GOAL.

People buy
into your
enthusiasm
before they buy
into you.

**The best thing about
the future is that it comes**

one
day
at
a
time.

—Abraham Lincoln

Have a deep sense of mission about who you are and what you intend to accomplish.

Remember, the most

well-adjusted people

are those who know how

to **BOU NCE** back.

Learn what is true in order to do what is right.

—Thomas Henry Huxley

To act
responsibly
you have
to take
leaps without
being sure.

—Daniel Ellsberg

No price is too high to pay for the privilege of owning yourself.

—Friedrich Wilhelm Nietzsche

It's a lot easier to prevent fires than to fight them.

dreams

We have but to
move in the
direction of our
dreams to meet
with a success
unexpected in
common hours.

—Henry David Thoreau

It is often your own bad habits that are the

biggest

obstacles

to achieving goals.

If you treat people right they will treat you right—ninety percent of the time.

—*Franklin Delano Roosevelt*

YOU MUST HAVE A SUBCONSCIOUS BELIEF IN YOUR OWN VALUE. THAT FEELING WILL BE CONVEYED WHEN YOU ARE TALKING WITH OTHERS.

Creative people carefully figure out what must be done. **Then, they do it.**

The more you think, the more time you have.

—Henry Ford

Consult not your fears but your hopes and your dreams. Think not about your frustrations, but about your unfulfilled potential. Concern yourself not with what you tried and failed in, but with what it is still possible for you to do.

—Pope John XXIII

WINNERS

are people who
continually make
small corrections in
their performances
until they get exactly
what they want.

The **art of negotiation** all comes down to knowing what you want and finding out what the other party wants.

Ask questions, listen, and be patient.

Be able to compromise!

You will reach an agreement.

I'm an idealist.

I don't know where I'm going but I'm on my way.

—Carl Sandburg